Letters from my Grandfather

Timeless Wisdom
For a Life Worth Living

Tim Jordan, M.D.

Letters from my Grandfather
Timeless Wisdom For a Life Worth Living
Tim Jordan, M.D.
Children & Families, Inc.

Published by Children & Families, Inc., St. Louis, MO
Copyright ©2018 Tim Jordan, M.D.

Names, characters, businesses, places, events and incidents are either the products of the author's imagination or used in a fictitious manner. Any resemblance to actual persons, living or dead, or actual events is purely coincidental.

Editor: Editor: Karyn Williams
Cover and Interior design: Davis Creative, DavisCreative.com

Library of Congress Cataloging-in-Publication Data
Library of Congress Control Number: 2018905737
Tim Jordan, M.D.
Letters from my Grandfather: Timeless Wisdom For a Life Worth Living
ISBN: 978-0-9771051-1-3
Library of Congress subject headings:
1. FAM033000 FAMILY & RELATIONSHIPS/Parenting/Parent & Adult Child
2. FAM043000 FAMILY & RELATIONSHIPS/Life Stages/Teenagers
3. FAM022000 FAMILY & RELATIONSHIPS/Parenting/Grandparenting

2018

This book is dedicated to any young adult who is wrestling with the challenges of finding their path and calling. Relax and enjoy the journey!

Table of Contents

Introduction. 1

The First Letter 5

17th Birthday: Negative Self-talk and Self-compassion 11

18th Birthday: One Right Path. 15

High School Graduation: Spiral of Beliefs. 21

1st Day of College: Go For The Roar. 25

19th Birthday: The Dot Theory 29

20th Birthday: Letting Go of Ropes 35

Start of Junior Year: The Power of Options. 39

21st Birthday: Set Your Own Bar. 43

Start of Senior Year: What Motivates You? 47

22nd Birthday: Mistakes Won't Mess Up Your Life. 51

College Graduation: Don't settle 55

23rd Birthday: Unrevealed Commitments 59

Final Letter: Open When Needed 63

Notes For Chapters 69

Acknowledgments 71

About the Author. 73

Introduction

Emma's grandfather died suddenly, and the loss hit her hard. He was her rock, her mentor, her shoulder to cry on. Her best friend was gone without warning, and she wondered how she would ever be able to get through life without him. Emma's parents were so caught up in their careers and schedules that they often weren't present, physically or emotionally. Grandpa was different; when she was with him, she always felt like the most important person in the world.

Grandpa had been there through countless skinned knees, friendship issues and lonely times when Emma's parents were too distracted to notice. He also had been there to celebrate her triumphs, new ideas and accomplishments. When she got upset about people or events, or became immersed in negative self-talk, he was always there to calm her down and get her back on track. Emma's heart was aching.

The memorial service was surreal; one minute he was with her, the next moment he was lying in a coffin, still and quiet. She felt like a big part of her went with him. So many memories flashed before her eyes, and they filled her with both love and longing.

She thought of their times together: getting picked up by him every day after school, walking up the creek and getting soaking wet and muddy, taking trips to the zoo, looking for new books at the library. Emma always looked forward to hearing his funny stories at extra-long tuck-ins whenever he babysat when her parents were out of town. She especially loved hearing stories about his childhood, and how he could relate to her present challenges. But she also remembered feeling so secure and happy just being in his presence, even when they were both quiet. It's a gift to have a friend with whom you can feel comfortable in those still moments.

It was her Grandpa who taught her to question everything. He was always asking 'why': why did she like art, love books and writing, like playing sports, dancing and being outdoors, enjoy time with friends, relish quiet alone time, or want to do well in school? He said if she was in charge of why she was doing something, it would help her get more out of it. He, of course, was right.

Emma's grandfather also taught her that whatever she did in this world mattered, and that her actions impacted others for better or for worse. He guided her to step in other people's shoes to see things from their perspective, and to develop greater empathy and respect for all human beings. It helped Emma understand her friends instead of judge them.

Emma learned that the best fruits are always out on the skinniest limbs; she needed to push herself out of her comfort zone and take risks. Through her Grandpa's examples and his encouragement, she learned that mistakes are opportunities to learn. He told stories of the lives of prominent people who had experienced trials and failures before they became successful, and this gave Emma hope during her own challenging times.

It was through his fun-natured teasing and banter that she learned to toughen up and not take things so personally. Grandpa helped her develop a good sense of humor, which gave her confidence, especially around boys.

Emma trusted her Grandpa with her innermost secrets because he was such a patient, nonjudgmental listener. She knew he understood her because he shared so many stories from his own life. She remembered coming home from school upset and confused about something that had happened, and he would calmly say,

"I want to hear what's upsetting you. Take all the time you need." Emma was going to miss bending his ear. Her Grandpa's unconditional love led the way for Emma to unconditionally love herself. She loved what she saw mirrored in his eyes when he looked at her, and she wanted to earn his love and respect. He modeled how to live positively, teaching by example and telling stories and metaphors that made sense to her. Grandpa was Emma's first and most important teacher and mentor.

When the memorial service finished, Emma's parents took her aside and handed her a shoebox with her name on top. Puzzled, she asked them what it was. They told her they found the box on her Grandpa's desk, and it was to be given to her upon his passing. It touched Emma so deeply that he had left her one last gift, even though she had no clue yet as to the contents of the box. But as she would discover, it was literally the gift that keeps on giving.

The First Letter

Opening up that box changed Emma's life forever. She was 16 when her grandfather died, about to enter 11th grade. She was in a fog as she drove home from the funeral with her parents, and she trudged up the stairs to her bedroom, lost in thought. Emma settled into bed with the shoebox before her. She wondered what this last gift from Grandpa would be, and hesitated to open it knowing the sadness that might ensue.

Emma was '16 going on 40' as her mom was fond of saying. People often described her as an 'old soul.' She always had seemed old for her age, more thoughtful and mature than her peers, and wise beyond her years. There was a knowingness about Emma; she understood things at a much deeper level than kids her age. It was hard for her to find like-minded peers, so she was kind of a loner at school, the kind of kid that everyone likes but doesn't get invited to sleepovers. Emma hated the drama that seemed to consume girls in her class and did her best to stay out of it. This distance kept her out of the loop because she wasn't privy to the latest gossip and scoops. Her grandpa had been the one person who really understood her, probably because they were so much alike.

Emma carefully untied the string that bound the box and with great anticipation, opened the lid. There was no present like a toy or book. What she saw was a stack of envelopes, tied together with a rubber band. Her curiosity heightened.

The letter on top had a short note that read: "Open this letter on the day of my funeral." Emma knew it was from her grandfather because of the writing. He had a style that was half print and half cursive, with a lot of abbreviations from his days as a doctor. Before she complied with the request, Emma glanced at the other letters in the pile and noticed the second one had a note that said, "Read on your 17th birthday." Awakened from her reverie, she quickly tore open letter number one, unfolded the page, and read what was to become the first of many such correspondences.

Dear Granddaughter,

First things first. I love you more than anything, more than the moon and the stars and the entire universe! And my love for you will never die, no matter how many seasons come and go. If you are reading this, I'm sure you have been through several days of emotions, and I wish I could have been there to comfort you. I'm truly sorry I won't be able to be with you physically from now on, but I thought perhaps I could be part of your journey through these heartfelt letters.

My death probably seems sudden to you, but I have known for a while that my life was coming to a close. I didn't tell you about my illness because I didn't want you to be worried about me, especially since there was nothing you could do about it. So, I had time to write you these letters that I hope you will read at the times written on the cover of each one.

Let's start this process with one of my favorite stories from the author Paul Villard[1].

A young girl, Sophia, was mesmerized by the new phone box in the kitchen, especially when her mom or dad talked to other people with it. She discovered that somewhere in that magical box lived an amazing person whose name was Information Please, and there was nothing she did not know.

One day when her parents were away at work, Sophia hit her finger with a hammer, and it really hurt. She picked up the phone receiver and said, "Information Please." A voice answered, "How can I help you?"

Sophia, crying big tears, responded, "I hurt my finger!"

"Is your mom home?" came the question.

"Nope, nobody here but me. I hit my thumb with a hammer, and it hurts."

"Can you open your icebox?"she asked. Sophia said she could. "Then chip off a little piece of ice, and hold it on your finger. That will stop the hurt. Be careful when you use the ice pick,"she noted. "And don't cry. You'll be alright."

After that, Sophia called Information Please for everything, from help with her math homework to asking where the Amazon River was located and what to feed a pet chipmunk she befriended in the park. One day Sophia called in tears because her pet canary had died, and Information Please did her best to console her.

"Why was it that birds should sing so beautifully and bring joy to whole families, only to end as a heap of feathers feet up on the bottom of a cage?"

The operator must have sensed her deep concern, for she quietly said, "Sophia, always remember that there are other worlds to sing in."

Somehow, she felt better.

Then, when she was 9 years old, Sophia moved across the country to Boston, and she missed her mentor tremendously. Information Please belonged in that old wooden box back at her old house. Yet, as she grew into her teens, the memories of those childhood conversations never really left her; often, in moments of doubt and perplexity, Sophia would recall the serene sense of security she had with Information Please. She appreciated now how very patient, understanding and kind she was to have wasted her time on a little girl.

Fast-forward 15 years when Sophia made a business trip to her hometown. Without really thinking, she dialed the operator and said, "Information please."

Miraculously, she heard the small, clear voice that she knew so well: "Information, how may I help?"

"Can you please tell me where on the map I can find the Amazon River?"

There was a pause, and then came that soft, reassuring voice, "I guess your finger has healed by now." It was her!

"So, it's really still you. I wonder if you have any idea how much you meant to me during all that time."

"I wonder", the operator replied, "if you know how much you meant to me? I never had any children, and I used to look forward to your calls. Silly, wasn't it?"

It didn't seem silly, but Sophia didn't say so. She told her how often she had thought of her over the years and asked if she could call her again when she came back to visit her sister.

"Please do. Just ask for Sue."

"Goodbye, Sue," Sophia said.

Just five months later Sophia was back in town, but a different voice answered. She asked for Sue.

"Are you a friend?" came the response.

"Yes," Sophia said. "An old friend."

"Then I'm sorry to have to tell you. Sue only had been working part-time the last few years because she was ill. She died five weeks ago."

Before Sophia could hang up, the operator said, "Wait a minute. Did you say your name was Sophia?"

"Yes it is."

"Well, Sue left a message for you. She wrote it down. Here it is: Tell her I still say there are other worlds to sing in. She'll know what I mean."

Sophia thanked her and hung up. She did know what Sally meant.

My dearest granddaughter, I love you, and I am so proud of who you are as a person. Know that I will always be with you in spirit, each and every step of the way.

Luv and hugs, and singing in another world,
Your Grandpa

P.S. Here's a quote to keep in mind any time you miss me:
"What we have once enjoyed we can never lose; all that we love deeply becomes a part of us." –Helen Keller

17th Birthday:

Negative Self-talk and Self-compassion

Everything was going well in her life, so why was Emma feeling so unsettled? Part of her problem was getting caught up in a lot of negative self-talk. Her Grandpa's letter could not have come at a better time. Knowing that she would be hearing from him on her birthday gave her comfort.

Dear Granddaughter,

Happiest 17th birthday! That's a lot of candles to blow out, signaling another step in your journey of becoming an adult. I'm guessing that you have a lot of things going on in your life as a high school junior, but I hope you are rising above the angst that can overcome people at your age. It's easy to get caught up in your busy schedule and neglect to take care of yourself.

I know how much you care about doing a good job at whatever you are involved with, so here are a few questions to ask yourself: Do you beat yourself up when you make mistakes or experience failures? Do you ever let discouragement cause you to procrastinate or to avoid doing things you know would be good for you? Do you tend to over-think every situation, ruminating worst-case scenarios until you feel overwhelmed?

The answer to these questions unfortunately was yes for Emma. She did tend to be hard on herself, and she had high expectations for herself too. She often compared herself to her peers, and almost always unfavorably.

Emma ruminated a lot, and the disquieting thoughts made it hard for her to fall asleep at night. Reading her grandfather's letter was already helping Emma feel calm.

If you answered yes to my questions, then here is my gift for your 17th birthday. Actually, it's a present you have to give to yourself, each and every day. The gift I am referring to is self-compassion.

Let me explain this phenomenon by telling you a story about the famous inventor Thomas Edison. It took Edison about three years to invent the light bulb; the biggest challenge was finding the right filament. He went through thousands of possible materials before discovering the winner: carbonized cotton thread. Before he died in 1931, Edison had 1,093 patents of his inventions. This quote of his describes how he overcame his mistakes.

"Results? Why, man, I have gotten lots of results! I am not discouraged, because every wrong attempt discarded is often a step forward. I have not failed. I've just found 10,000 ways that won't work."

Thomas Edison did not allow his mistakes and failures to discourage him. His level of self-compassion must have been incredibly high to keep him going despite thousands of setbacks with his experiments. Let me explain how you can use self-compassion in your life.

There are three components of self-compassion: self-kindness, a sense of common humanity and mindfulness. Self-kindness involves talking to yourself in a soothing, gentle way, much like a person who loves you unconditionally would, like me for instance. When you catch yourself in negative self-talk, ask yourself, "What would Grandpa say to me right now?" Or imagine what your best friend or parents would say. They would use encouraging words like, "It's OK; it's just a mistake. You'll do better next time. I love you no matter what." This is especially valuable when you make mistakes or get frustrated.

When faced with challenges or painful experiences, it also helps tremendously to understand that you aren't the only person who is struggling, that no one is perfect, and to connect your experience with countless others before you who have faced challenges and persevered. It's comforting to remind yourself that you are not alone.

Finally, self-compassion involves using mindfulness to bring awareness to what you are experiencing and feeling without getting caught up in it and overreacting. You learn to notice without judgment.

Here's another great story to illustrate self-compassion. A man was very proud of his garden, and every day he made the journey to his shed where he filled up two buckets with water. He would then walk along the pathway that led to his flower beds to water his plants. One of his buckets was a brand-new, shiny red pail, and the other was a very old, dilapidated bucket. The new bucket was very proud of itself for being able to carry a full load of water without spilling a drop, whereas the shabby old one had holes in it that allowed water to spill out all along the route. The shabby bucket told her friend that she felt ashamed of itself for the leakage, but was comforted in knowing that the gardener still found some use for her. One day the gardener overheard this conversation between the buckets and decided to teach them a lesson. When he had finished his watering, he asked them to look carefully at the path on their way back to the shed. What they noticed was that all along the side of the path where the new bucket was carried was just bare earth. But along the other side where the gardener carried the leaky old pail, there was a row of fresh spring flowers. The old bucket's perceived weakness actually had been a gift to others. The kind gardener modeled self-compassionate thinking for the leaky bucket.

One last story to help with keeping yourself positive and encouraged: A young girl went to her grandfather one day because she was having a hard time not dwelling on negative thoughts. "Ah," said the grandfather, "I know just what you are experiencing because I have the same thing going on inside of me. It's like there are two wolves in my head. One wolf is very negative, discouraging, pessimistic, jealous and angry. The second wolf is kind, encouraging, positive, loving, optimistic and peaceful. Those two wolves are constantly battling over who is going to win." The girl asked, "Which wolf wins, papa?" The grandfather replied, "The wolf that wins is the one that I feed the most."

What you say to yourself about yourself is important, especially when you are struggling. From this day forward, whenever you experience a challenging or painful event, talk to yourself using compassionate words of encouragement, empathy and reassurance. Do not allow any one event to define you. Bring yourself to the present moment by practicing mindfulness, and watch as your worries float away. Catch yourself when you start to ruminate and gently redirect your thinking. And be sure to feed your positive wolf!

Be as kind to yourself as I would be to you.
Love, Grandpa

18th Birthday:

◡𝓂◡

One Right Path

Half-way through her senior year of high school, Emma had looked forward to celebrating her 18th birthday, especially since it was when she could read her grandfather's next letter. She felt as if she was on an emotional roller coaster; some days she couldn't wait to get out of high school, other days she grew sad thinking about moving away from friends and family. The pressure was intensifying about college, and Emma got overwhelmed thinking about applications and college visits. So, she did what many young people do at that age; she procrastinated and stayed busy and distracted so she didn't have to think about it. Growing up seemed to be hard and stressful. She rushed to her room after school and opened up her grandfather's letter.

Dear Emma,

Happy 18th birthday! I am sure you are growing into a powerful young woman who is in the process of figuring out what to do after you graduate. I wish I could be there to support you through the process, but this note will have to suffice.

I had noticed in the past several years that you and your friends were getting stressed out about your futures. It seems like there is this belief out there that starting in middle school, kids should know the choice of university they will attend, their major in college, their career choice, and the need to have their whole life figured out. I wonder if you are getting anxious about decisions for next year and beyond. Let me see if I can lessen your fears with a few stories.

Nathan Sawaya loved building Legos as a kid[2][3]. When he was 9, his parents refused to let him get a dog, and he channeled his disappointment by building a life-sized pooch with Legos. He says it was an 'aha' moment, realizing he could build from his imagination versus following the instructed design. From that day forward, if he thought about becoming an astronaut, he built himself a rocket; if he wanted to be a rock star, he constructed a guitar.

When he went to college and then law school, he kept a box of Legos hidden under his bed that he periodically brought out. He moved on to become a successful merger and acquisitions attorney but continued to create with his Legos. He began to accept commissions for his Lego sculptures, and on the day his artwork website crashed from excessive traffic, he decided to make a change. He walked into his boss's office the next day and told him, "I'm going to play with toys full time." Since then, he has travelled worldwide displaying and selling his Lego pieces. He typically has around 4 million Legos in his design studio. Nathan found his passion.

I love how Nathan was able to veer off of a more typical path and make his own way. I worry that our culture has brainwashed your generation to believe that there is only one prescribed path that everyone is supposed to follow; i.e. get good grades in school, go to a top university, and land a high-paying job. The truth is that almost no one at point A at age 18 knows what they will be doing at point Z at age 50, and that no adult travels along a straight path. It's also true that almost no adult travelled on a straight line from point A to point Z, where they are in their career as middle-aged adults. People tend to zig-zag their way to finding their life's work. Nathan Sawaya is a good example of someone who found his life's work after some early detours.

The nail that sticks up gets hammered down.

Anyone who tries to veer off of the expected path is pressured to follow the crowd. There are numerous ways to get to your destiny, so you'll need to let go of some powerful cultural conditioning. I once heard a story about a man who was on an African safari when he noticed a herd of elephants walking down a road in orderly fashion led by a trainer. The only thing linking the animals together was a thin chain attached around their front right legs. The man asked the trainer how such a weak chain could hold these powerful beasts. The trainer's answer was revealing. "We used the same chain to restrict their movements when they were young, so they were taught to believe that the chain would constrain them even though they now are bigger and stronger and could easily break free." That is the power of cultural conditioning.

So, here's what I want you to remember, my granddaughter. There is no one right path for everyone, and it's OK and normal to not know your whole life story as a young adult. Don't let other people limit your thinking or your dreams. Listen to the advice of adults who care about you, but filter it through what you feel is right for you. That's what the eminent architect Frank Lloyd Wright did.

Wright remembered his traditional, stolid uncle taking him for a long walk across a snow-covered field when he was 9 years old. When they got to the edge of the field, his uncle told him to look back over both of their tracks. He told him to notice how Frank's footprints meandered back and forth, from the trees on one side to looking at cattle on the other side and then across the way when he was throwing sticks. The uncle's path came straight across, directly to his goal. He told Frank to never forget that lesson. Frank didn't, but not as his uncle had imagined. He decided then and there to never miss out on most things in life as his uncle had. Frank Lloyd Wright decided to forge his own path.

Jennifer Lawrence carved out an atypical path to become an Oscar-winning actress[4]. Jennifer was constantly performing as a kid, inventing stories just to invent them. "I didn't know I was an actor, I just thought I was a weirdo," she said. Her antics were a way to hide the fact that she struggled as a poor student, was hyperactive, and never felt like she fit in. She badgered her parents to take her to New York, where she luckily was discovered by a modeling scout. They had her read a script, and it changed her life. "I read the script and I knew exactly what it would look like if someone felt that way." Jennifer got an overwhelming feeling that acting was what she was meant to do. She dropped out of middle school at 14, and without any acting training, got a small role in a sitcom, where her parents saw her happy and focused for the first time. She won an Oscar nomination for best actress for her first movie role in *Winter's Bone* at age 18, became the lead in the *Hunger Games* series at age 21, and has made two movies a year since the age of 20. At the age of 14 she knew what she wanted. "I wanted to forge my own path," she said. "I found what I wanted to do, and I did not want anything to get in the way of it. Even my friends from the age of 14 on were less important than my career." Jennifer Lawrence is a great example of someone who veered off of the prescribed path to create her own journey.

I strongly encourage you to interview every adult you know, as well as those who have careers you find interesting. Ask them what their vision for their vocation was when they were your age. Have them describe how their career path unfolded. Read biographies of anyone you find interesting or unique. I'm certain you will find as many stories as there are people you interview.

Emma, my birthday wish for you is that you avoid getting sucked into your peer's stress and instead choose to go through the college process with courage and peace. Don't blindly follow a certain path and take whatever time you need to figure out what's right for you.

Love, Grandpa

High School Graduation:

Spiral of Beliefs

Things had fallen into place for Emma, and she was feeling confident about her choice of college. Her senior year ended well with good friends, good grades and a better relationship with her parents. She knew her grandfather would have been proud of her as she walked up to receive her diploma, and he would love the person she had become. Emma decided to read his letter before she left for the ceremony so that she could carry his words and memory with her on this special day.

Dear Emma,

Congratulations! I wish I could be there to watch you cross the stage and accept your high school diploma, but this letter will just have to do the trick. Let's start with this quote by George Kelly.

"No one needs to be a victim of their own biography."

As you walk off the stage and into the next phase of your life, you might want to step back for a moment and consider what you want to bring with you from your past. Whether you are aware of it or not, you have made decisions about yourself, your relationships and your life based on your experiences; some healthy and some not. Some of these beliefs you will want to pack with you to college, and others you will want to leave behind or reframe. I can explain with a true story.

Annie had three best friends through sixth grade, but in seventh grade, they started to not call her on the weekends. She would see pictures of them at sleepovers on Instagram, and when she asked if they were still her friends, they would tell her of course and not to worry about it. But they never called. Annie felt confused, excluded and sad. She asked herself questions like, "Why don't my friends ever call me? Why are they leaving me out?" And then she would answer those questions with her own private logic that she was possibly weird, annoying, not good enough, not cool enough, or not pretty or thin enough. Annie became more insecure and self-conscious, and she had a hard time trusting people and opening up to friends. This in turn didn't allow peers to get to know the real Annie, and so she often became the third wheel. Her thoughts became more solid beliefs: "I'm not important. I'm invisible. I can't trust anyone. I'm not lovable or loved. I'm alone and worthless." She became a victim of this spiral of negative beliefs.

I'm sure you have experienced some tough times with friends or life along the way, so it's really important that you become aware of any limiting beliefs you may be carrying around in your head, because they will affect how you act. Have you ever asked yourself questions like:

Why do friends keep leaving me out?

Why do I have such a hard time trusting people?

Why do I keep ending up in unhealthy, unfulfilling relationships?

Why do I feel so awkward around new people and groups?

Why do I doubt myself so often?

If so, you probably have some negative beliefs inside of you that need to see the light of awareness.

The belief that Emma connected with was the one about trusting people, and she realized that it stemmed from her experience of losing friends back in middle school. Despite having made good friends in high school, she still occasionally felt the old anxiety about being left out and was a little worried about creating a new friend group at college.

Here's another great quote for you to chew on: "I am not what has happened to me, I am what I choose to become." Carl Jung

Once you become aware of these thoughts, then you must make better sense of your experience. Annie had to understand that it was not her fault that her friends ditched her, and it didn't mean anything about who she was as a person. Like Annie, instead of making negative assumptions and getting caught up in thought distortions triggered by your spiral of beliefs, you can learn to catch yourself and do a reality check.

Here's other quick story:

Suppose you have $86,400 in your account and someone steals $10 from you; would you be so upset with them that you'd be willing to throw all of the $86,390 away in hopes of getting back at the person who took your $10? Or move on? Right, you'd move on. See, we have 86,400 seconds in every day, so don't let someone's negative 10 seconds ruin the rest of the 86,390. Don't sweat the small stuff; life is bigger than that.

This was definitely something Emma needed to work on, because she still at times let other people's snide comments affect her.

I wonder if you have ever allowed critical words from a peer or some form of disrespect ruin your day and start this spiral of beliefs? If so, you might want to remind yourself that these past experiences or any such future ones are not worth your fretting over and causing you to doubt yourself. Confucius once said, "To be wronged is nothing unless you continue to remember it." Make other people's opinions of you 'small stuff' and focus on the positives from the other 86,390 seconds of each day.

"We cannot control the parade of negative thoughts marching through our minds. But we can choose which ones we will give attention to. Picture your thoughts as people passing by the front of your home. Just because they're walking by doesn't mean you have to invite them in." –Gladys Edmunds

I love this quote. It reminds me to focus on what I have control over, and to let go of things I don't control. Annie, and you, must become the author of your story instead of the victim of your biography. Use this summer before you go off to college to reflect and do some soul-searching about this issue, and make conscious decisions about letting go of old, limiting mental baggage. I'll leave you with one more fitting quote until the next letter you will read before you leave for college.

"The soul becomes dyed with the colors of its thoughts." –Marcus Aurelius

I am so proud of you!
Congratulations, Grandpa

1st Day of College:

cne

Go For The Roar

Emma settled onto her bed and brought out her next letter. She had arrived at college that morning and spent several hours moving into her dorm room with the help of her parents. Then there came an awkward pause. Her mom started crying, her dad held back tears, and Emma put on a brave face and told her parents she was fine and it was time for them to go. As their car drove off, Emma was filled with a mix of emotions: excitement, fear, and anticipation. Her roommate hadn't arrived yet, so she took this quiet time to read her grandfather's words.

Dear College Student,

As I imagine you sitting on your bed in your dorm, I can see you back at your first day of kindergarten, and it makes me smile. You've come a long way baby, as they say. I can't imagine how excited and nervous you must be. It's a big day and a big step in your life, but I know you are ready for it. I want you to feel open to new people and experiences, and for the possibility of reinventing yourself. The only thing that could possibly hold you back from attaining this is your fears: fears of making mistakes, fear of failure, fear of disappointing people or fear of the unknown. So, here's one of my favorite stories to help you through any worries:

Lions in Africa have an interesting method of hunting gazelle. The young lions hide in the brush downwind from a herd of gazelle, and when they are all set, the oldest male lion in the pride goes to work. He is weak, can't run and has no teeth, but he can still growl with the best of them. The old guy sits up and roars loudly; the gazelle hear him and smell his scent, and where do you think they run? They head away from the sounds and right into the teeth of the younger lions, who eat them up.

The moral of the story: in your life, when you hear the roar (feel your fear), the tendency is to run away from it or avoid the situation. This makes your anxiety rise, making it harder to proceed this time and in the future. You metaphorically get eaten up by your fears. Instead, I encourage you to go for the roar, to go towards and through your fears because you will find that what you were afraid of doesn't have as many 'teeth' as you thought.

I love that metaphor. You are old enough now to recall times when you were anxious about upcoming exams, auditions, sporting events or meeting new groups of peers. The truth is that what you were afraid of almost always never occurred. If something did, it wasn't as bad as you thought, and you handled it. That should give you the courage to go for the roar with future situations, because the truth about Emma is that you have been there before and have handled every challenge you've faced.

"I've been absolutely terrified every moment of my life, and I've never let it keep me from doing a single thing that I wanted to do." –Georgia O'Keefe

Everyone has fears, and it's important to face them with courage and not let worries cause you to miss out on opportunities. Every time you go for the roar, you add another building block to your confidence level. Like Georgia O'Keefe, you are going to be confronted with fears, and you need to get in the habit of pushing through them.

"Twenty years from now, you will be more disappointed by the things you didn't do than by the ones you did. "So throw off the bowlines. Sail away from the safe harbor. Catch the trade winds in your sails. Explore, dream, discover." Mark Twain

Let me tell you two more stories about people who went for the roar.

Joy Mangano was scared when she put all of her life savings into creating a prototype kitchen mop she called the Miracle Mop. She was terrified when she convinced the QVC producer to allow her to go on live TV to sell the mop herself. Joy went for the roar and has sold millions of her products since. Watch the movie *Joy* about her life story; it's very inspiring.

Scott had several interviews at a top brokerage firm in New York, and the head of the company acknowledged him for how calm he was throughout the process. Scott recalled that at age 11, he had a job cutting the grass at his dad's office each week, until one day he skipped to play ball with his friends. When he arrived the next week to mow the grass, he found it was already done. His dad told him he assumed he had quit and he hired another kid.

It took six months of hounding before he got his dad to reconsider, but it required him going to his dad's office to interview for the job. Scott remembers feeling intimidated sitting across the desk from his 6'4" father, who asked him questions about why he wanted the job, where he saw himself with the job in one to two years, and his level of motivation and responsibility. Scott's dad let him come back, but first he had to prove his dedication by folding boxes in the factory for two months before he was allowed to cut the grass. Scott told the firm's president after that interview with his dad, nothing was ever that hard again. He went for the roar and has never looked back.

My dear Emma, I know how much courage you have in you because I saw you face challenges so many times growing up. Every time you face your fears and push through them, you gain confidence, and more confidence translates to more willingness to take risks, be bold and creative, and to stretch out of your comfort zone.

Entrepreneurs have this spirit, and so can you if you embrace the notion of going for the roar.

Know that as you face new obstacles and challenges in the coming months and years, you have what it takes to triumph. I'm always there looking over your shoulder, so you are never alone. Enjoy college, sweetie!

Love, Grandpa

19th Birthday:

᷑ᒿᑲ᷑

The Dot Theory

After two months in college, Emma felt fairly settled socially. She got along well with her roommate and had made several other good friends on her floor. What was unsettling was her lack of direction. Many of her peers had decided on their majors, yet Emma didn't have a clue what career path she wanted to pursue. She felt confused, frustrated and behind. On her 19th birthday, Emma waited to read her grandfather's letter until her roommate was asleep.

Dear Emma,

Happy 19th birthday! I guess this is the first birthday you have experienced away from home, so I hope you have made some good friends to celebrate with. That first semester away from home can be daunting with so many changes. I hope you've started to develop a new support system of friends.

I wonder what field of study you will eventually pursue. You have always been so well-rounded and good at a lot of things, so sometimes that can make it harder to choose. I remember even back in middle school, you were feeling pressure about knowing your career choice, so I thought I'd offer you a little advice and reassurance about the process of discovering your calling. Here's a good quote to get us started.

"If you move in the direction of your passions, opportunities tend to appear that you couldn't have imagined and that weren't otherwise there." –Joseph Campbell

Do you remember one of our favorite activities we used to play together? It was connect the numbered dot drawings; you look at a page full of dots and have no idea what the final picture will become. You start connecting the dots, and after a while, a picture starts to emerge. It didn't matter that you had no clue at the start about what the final picture would be. As long as you persisted in connecting the dots, an image would develop.

Those drawings inspired me to create what I call my Dot Theory. This theory is a different way of discovering your life's work. Let me relate a story from my life that will make this concept clearer.

Growing up with five younger sisters gave me lots of experience with being a diaper changer, playmate, babysitter, homework tutor and shoulder to cry on. I'm sure my love of taking care of girls began there.

My favorite summers were spent as a camp counselor during middle and early high school, further entrenching my love for working with kids. In addition, I volunteered as a counselor at a day camp for children with cerebral palsy and fell in love with them. I also had the opportunity to hang out with kids with hearing impairments my senior year of high school, and I became enamored with kids who were deaf; they had a unique and fun energy about them that I loved to be around. Over the next 10 years, I accumulated more related experiences, including: working with deaf children at the Missouri School for the Deaf, a moonlighting job for two years as the medical director of a residential facility for severely handicapped children, and finally two years of fellowship training in developmental and behavioral pediatrics.

With my training finally complete, I moved back to the St. Louis area to start my career. I began looking for opportunities to use my fellowship training, starting with the United Cerebral Palsy Center where I had worked those two summers. I made an appointment to meet with the executive director, and when I walked into his office, we realized we both knew each other. I had volunteered with Kevin at the day camp years before. He hired me to be the facility's part-time medical director, a position I held for about 10 years. That story came full circle.

I would suggest that instead of becoming stressed about figuring out your life's work, just be open to dots. Dots are any experiences that cross your path that you seem drawn to. If it seems like it would be fun or it just seems like the right thing to do, then by all means pursue it. Dots can look like a lot of things: a class, a job, volunteer work, internships, traveling, reading a biography, joining a club or group, trying a new activity, or having a cup of coffee with an adult you find interesting. This quote by Steve Chandler describes this process well: "Listen to the clues. The next time you feel real joy, stop and think. Pay attention. Because joy is the universe's way of knocking on your mind's door. Hello in there. Is anyone home? Can I leave a message? Good! The message is that you are happy, and that means that you are in touch with your purpose."

I didn't volunteer at the cerebral palsy center as a 15-year-old because someday I wanted to be a developmental and behavioral pediatrician. I did it because it seemed like it would be fun, and I liked working with kids. From my story, you can see how that picture in my life slowly but surely evolved, one seemingly unconnected experience at a time.

Remember how much we loved watching those Muppet movies? Jim Henson, the creator of the Muppets, has an interesting dot story[5]. He loved watching movies as a kid and would reenact scenes with his friends, building elaborate props and costumes. He also listened to comedians on radio shows, especially Edgar Bergen and his dummy Charlie McCarthy. In high school, Jim designed and built sets and created posters for the drama club, and he joined the puppetry club. At end of his senior year, he got a job at a CBS affiliate TV station manipulating marionettes for a children's show. Even then Jim considered himself more of an artist and designer, but if puppetry got him into TV, that was fine with him.

In college, he studied stage design and art, and when he took a new puppetry class with a novice teacher, he ended up taking over the class. Jim got a job doing puppetry for an NBC station, and gradually received more attention and air time. All the time he was in college, he never took puppetry seriously; he saw it as a means to an end, i.e. work in TV and movies as a set designer.

"Puppetry did not seem like a thing a grown-up man works at for a living," he said. Looking back at his career, Jim stated, "It's certainly not a career that you would plan. You would not decide to become a puppeteer. I had no desire to become a performer; my interest was in TV, film and art; puppetry combined them all. I thought I would only do puppetry a short time." Jim Henson just kept embracing the opportunities that came his way, which culminated in him becoming an internationally acclaimed puppeteer, film maker, documentarian and co-creator of Sesame Street.

You know how my favorite basketball team was the San Antonio Spurs? Here's another great dot story that involves their assistant coach[6]. Five-foot six-inch Becky Hammon's only basketball scholarship offer was to Colorado State University. She left college four years later as the all-time leading scorer in the WAC conference history, male or female. She was not drafted by any team in the WNBA but was able to earn a spot onto the New York Liberty team. By her fifth year, she led the team in scoring before tearing her ACL. She subsequently was traded to San Antonio, where she played well. Becky was so crushed she was not selected to the U.S. Olympic basketball team in 2008 that she chose to become a Russian citizen, much to the dismay of her colleagues. "I know I can take a lot of crap when I follow my heart. I proved I'm not afraid to take a risk. And I risked a lot, like my reputation. People said terrible things about me."

On the plane ride home from the Olympics, she found herself seated next to Greg Popovich, coach of the San Antonio Spurs. He'd had an interest in Russia since his days as the Soviet specialist at the Air Force Academy. He was impressed with her guts and the way she seized the day. Becky tore her ACL again in 2013 right before the Spurs began training camp, and Popovich invited her to have unlimited access to the team because of his respect for her. Two years later, she became the first woman to coach an NBA team in its premier summer league. "My journey has been divinely orchestrated, with one step leading to another," she said. She could not have explained the dot theory any better.

Mick Fleetwood struggled in school with undiagnosed learning disabilities and felt completely lost[7]. His only passion was drumming. Fortunately, his father had taken the unconventional route of pursuing a writing career, so he understood Mick's dilemma. Mick's epiphany moment came when he visited his sister in London and she took him to a jazz club. It was like a whole new world of opportunities opened up for him, and he knew he had found his dream. The vision of becoming a musician kept him going in school, but his real commitment was to become a drummer. At age 16, he told his parents he wanted to leave school and pursue his dream, and they gave him their blessing. Several years later he formed the band Fleetwood Mac, and the rest, as they say, is history.

Jim Henson didn't sign onto doing marionettes on TV because he wanted to become a puppeteer. Becky Hammon's reason for playing for the Russian Olympic basketball team wasn't because she wished to coach for an NBA team. Mick Fleetwood went to the jazz club on a whim. They all just did what seemed like fun at the time, and life did the rest. That is how life can work for you as well.

My dearest granddaughter, I believe that this is the way you will find your life's work. You don't need to get stressed out and overwhelmed because you don't know the answer right now. Dismiss the pressure, be open to dots that present themselves, follow your heart, and then allow the picture of your life and career to unfold, marvelously, in its own way and in its own time. I'll leave you with one more related quote from eminent psychologist Joseph Campbell.

"Follow your bliss. You put yourself on a kind of track that has been there all the while, waiting for you, and the life you ought to be living is the one you are living. When you can see that, you begin to meet people who are in your field of bliss, and they open doors to you. Follow your bliss and don't be afraid, and doors will open where you didn't know they were going to be."

Relax and enjoy the ride.
Love, Grandpa

20ᵗʰ Birthday:

⌒ɴ⌒

Letting Go of Ropes

As Emma neared the end of her sophomore year of college, she still hadn't decided on her major, and the pressure was mounting to do so. Everyone offered her advice, whether or not it was solicited: her parents, aunts and uncles, grandparents, professors and peers. This led Emma to feel confused and pulled in many different directions. She had always been a sensitive girl who was conscious of not wanting to disappoint people. Emma felt stuck and hoped her grandfather's letter on her 20th birthday would offer her some peace of mind.

Dear Granddaughter,

I so wish I could be there to celebrate your 20th birthday. I imagine you are facing the challenge of choosing your major if you haven't already, so I thought I'd add my two cents. I hope you aren't getting overwhelmed with all of the good-intentioned suggestions from those who love and care about you. It can be daunting to sift through everyone's advice and know what's right for you. As you know, I used to talk with groups of high school and college women about finding their calling. Let me share with you an exercise I used to do with them that might give you some clarity.

I would place a woman in the middle of the room, let's call her Grace, and blindfold her. There would be four ropes attached to a belt around her waist, extending 10 feet to each corner of the room, and held tightly by four people. Grace's challenge was to see how fast she could pick up four small objects that were placed around the room that represented what she most desired in life. Her 'guides' could use the ropes and their voices to help her accomplish the task. Ready, set, go!

It normally took people about a minute and a half to pick up the four articles, and they'd feel pretty good about their accomplishment. They would then redo the challenge with a few changes. The second time, I removed her covering and instead blindfolded the four helpers, so that they were now blind and mute. I told Grace she could now see, she was limitless, and could do whatever she wanted to grab the objects; ready, set, go! As it usually happened, she dragged her cohorts to the four corners of the room, barking instructions along the way, and completed the job in around 40 seconds. Everyone would clap for her, and then we'd process the exercise.

The four items represented her happiness, a successful career, finding a soul mate and contentment. I'd ask how Grace could have collected the objects in about 10 seconds, and the room would go silent; no one had a clue. Then, I'd drop the bombshell. "Why didn't you take off the belt?" I always heard a bunch of excuses like how I hadn't told her she could, which I would refute. I'd remind everyone that my instructions were that she was limitless and could do whatever she wanted. I performed that exercise for 30 years, and no one ever thought to remove the belt.

This is a great metaphor for where you are at this stage of your life. The guides represent your parents, coaches, relatives and teachers you have relied upon to keep you safe and offer guidance when you have insufficient life experience. As you enter adulthood, it's crucial that you start to let go of the ropes and take on more responsibility for your life. The ropes that were initially guidelines can become limitations, and we are often unaware of how they prevent our success. You may have become programmed to depend on others for making important life decisions and knowing what's right for you and your happiness.

There are many reasons why people don't 'take off their ropes.' People often have been conditioned to overestimate what they need from others and to underestimate what they can do for themselves, especially if their parents micromanaged them throughout childhood. For some young adults, it's easier to blame others instead of taking responsibility.

There are also many kinds of 'ropes' that can prevent people from taking charge of their lives. Some common ones are: fear of failure, fear of the unknown, the old beliefs I told you about in your high school graduation letter, a low level of confidence and grit, or worrying about looking good and not standing out. For many women, not wanting to disappoint people or lose approval is a huge rope to overcome. Let me tell you a good story to show you what I mean:

The egg of an eagle somehow found its way into a barn where a hen was hatching her eggs. In due time, the eaglet was hatched with the other chicks. As time passed, she began to experience a longing to fly. She asked her mother, the hen, "When shall I learn to fly?"

The poor hen had no clue how to train her to fly, but was ashamed to confess this to the eaglet. She told her, "Not yet, my child. I shall teach you when you are ready." Months passed, and the young eagle began to suspect her mother did not know how to fly. But she could not get herself to break free and fly on her own because her keen longing to fly had become confused with the gratitude she felt towards the bird who had hatched her.

I know how much you love your parents, and I would encourage you to always listen to the advice from people who you respect. But I would then have some alone, quiet time to run their suggestions through your own filter: "Does their counsel fit for me? Is it in alignment with what I have decided is right for me?" By this time in your life, there needs to be a transition where you now trust that *you* know what's best for you, not others.

Emma, become aware of what ropes you are holding onto that are preventing you from creating the life you want, especially the one about not wanting to disappoint other people. That kind of awareness is 90 percent of the battle. Take some steps, big or small, toward more responsibility. Notice how you feel when you let go of a rope and follow your intuition and heart. Compare that to what you feel when you let others control your destiny: resentment, anger, frustration and controlled. Being responsible also means being free, so focus on the reward of freedom to live your life how you want.

Let go of any limiting ropes and spend time reflecting, and you will find the answers to your questions. In your heart, you will know what field of study to pursue. I hope this note brings you peace of mind and the confidence to believe in yourself. Keep enjoying 'dots' and enjoy the journey.

Best wishes, Grandpa

Start of Junior Year:

⟋⟍

The Power of Options

Emma had chosen psychology as her major and was enjoying the classes tremendously. She wondered sometimes what kind of job she would get after graduation, and even what kind of psychology she might study in grad school. Emma knew she wanted to have a career that would allow her to directly help people, like her grandfather did for her. It was time for her next letter, and as always, she looked forward to hearing her grandfather's words.

Dear Emma,

Can you believe you are in the second half of college already? I hope this letter finds you happy and more settled. Even if you have chosen a major, remind yourself that you always have lots of options to follow. Let me share with you some great advice I got when I was your age from a mentor that helped me with career decisions.

At the end of my second year of college, it was time to choose a major, and I was stuck. I had known since I was a kid that I wanted to work with children, but I couldn't decide between becoming a teacher or a pediatrician. I had taken prerequisites for both majors over the first two years, but it was time to decide on my future.

I went in to talk to the pre-med adviser, Brother John Donohoo. I had met with him a few times in the past when I felt discouraged, and I always left his office feeling on top of the world. On this occasion, he gave me some advice that changed my life.

Brother John told me that I'd make a great teacher because of how much I loved working with kids, but that after some time I might get bored or restless, at which point I might elect to become a principal. But he felt that there weren't too many more options on that track. He said that attaining an M.D. would give me credentials that would open up countless possibilities for me down the road. He encouraged me to choose a major that would create the most opportunities. That is the main reason why I chose to become a physician, and I've never regretted it.

My M.D. credentials became invaluable over the years when I tried to get books published, get a radio show, get hired to give presentations for parents and professionals, or land interviews for various positions. They really have opened up doors that might not have been there without my background, and they've allowed me to pursue so many interesting career paths.

My wish for you is to keep an open mind to what I see as endless possibilities to use whatever expertise you acquire. We all have choices, and we all have the freedom to make our lives the way we desire. Don't ever assume a victim mentality. I'm going to tell you stories of some fascinating people who kept their options open and created remarkable lives. An interesting young woman named Bobbi was someone who didn't fall into the victim mindset[8].

Bobbi changed colleges twice in two years, following first a boyfriend and then friends. She came home after her second year and told her parents, "School is not for me." Her mom asked what she was passionate about and Bobbi said, "Makeup." They researched colleges that had studies in this field and Bobbi went with her gut and settled on Emerson College. The college allowed this young woman to formulate her own concentration, and she took classes in theater, TV, film, photography and makeup. She says now, "I left with a B.A. in fine arts in makeup with a minor in photography, but what I really left with was the knowledge that it was all up to me."

Bobbi Brown was able to create a successful cosmetics company, Bobbi Brown Cosmetics, because she had learned to be the captain of her fate. She created her own options. Here are some quotes from her that you might put up in your room for inspiration.

"Everything in life, everything, is what you put into it. There are so many options for how you live your life and make a career for yourself."

"If you can identify and stick with something you're genuinely passionate about, you're ahead of the game. You'll figure out how to make money once you figure out what you love to do."

Sharon Long worked a lot of jobs in her 20s and 30s, and at age 40, she went to college to get an art/sculpting degree[9]. She ended up enjoying an anthropology class, especially the forensics side of it. A professor noticed she was good at art, and asked, "Why don't you try making faces?" Here's how Sharon describes her love of making molds of skulls: "I get totally psyched into what I am doing. I keep the skull in front of me for a while, just looking at it and forming it in my mind. I kind of meditate about their life and, depending on their age, I try to go by how I was at that age. I research the time period and try to think about them as a person like me, because they were, once upon a time. It doesn't even seem like time goes by; I forget to eat, forget to get up, forget to drink water. Everything just goes into suspension. Fifteen hours later, I have a face."

By going back to college, following her passion and keeping her options open, Sharon became an eminent forensic artist.

Dorothy Warburton won an essay contest at age 14, and the prize was a book about women scientists[10]. The stories inspired her to think that someday she, too, could accomplish that. Dorothy taught herself to type because she imagined being a secretary to a great scientist. After earning a Ph.D., she took a job as a research associate in the OB-GYN department at Columbia University where her husband worked. No one was interested in the problem of miscarriages, so Dorothy began researching the issue despite no initial support. Eventually, she got backing from the director of the hospital, and Dorothy developed one of the first genetic diagnostic laboratories in the country. She kept the window of opportunity open instead of settling.

Nicole Hanton overcame incredible challenges growing up[11]. She had an alcoholic mom who shipped her off at age 12 to live with her dad who was a drug addict and subsequently molested her. She returned to her mom and spent her teen years taking care of her younger brother and her mother. Her saving grace was Lorrie, the mother of her best friend, who became the supportive adult she craved. Nicole found out that this woman had grown up with abusive parents, yet had survived and flourished. One day Lorrie gave her advice that changed her life: "You know, your life is like a train, Nicole, and you're riding down a certain set of tracks," she said. "But here's the incredible thing: even though your childhood has gone one way, you can jump that set of tracks and follow your own tracks."

Nicole realized she could make her own choices that were different than those of her parents. It gave her hope for her future. Today, Nicole works for a rape crisis center and with child protective services, where she shares her mentor Lorrie's invaluable advice.

Never allow yourself to feel like you have no options. Use the examples of Bobbi Brown, Sharon Long, Dorothy Warburton and Nicole Hanton to inspire you to think big and outside the box of typical possibilities. When you hit one of those forks in the road where you have to choose a field of study or a job, consider which opportunity will provide you with the most potential, and go in that direction. My dear Emma, make your life incredible!

Love, Grandpa

21ˢᵗ Birthday:

⌒*ᴍ*⌒

Set Your Own Bar

Emma approached her 21st birthday with both excitement and some anxiety. She was excited at being classified more as an adult, and being able to go to bars and order drinks. She liked the idea of feeling more grown up. Her concern came from knowing she still had a hard time making decisions for herself. The 'approval rope' was the hardest for her to let go of, and the inability to think for herself often left her confused and paralyzed. Emma constantly doubted herself, and she had a habit of over-thinking things to the point of getting overwhelmed. She sat on a park bench at the edge of a pond to read the letter her grandfather had addressed, "Read on your 21st birthday."

Dear Emma,

Welcome to the world of adulthood! I hope you are having a great day on this, your 21st birthday. I wonder if you are seeing yourself more like an adult these days. You were always an old soul and seemed older than your years. I mentioned in my letter on your 20th birthday that it was time to start letting go of any 'ropes' that might be holding you back; remember that? Another big piece of growing up is to set your own expectations for yourself. Let me tell you stories of three women and how they learned to set their own bar.

Mia Hamm, the most decorated women's soccer player in U.S. history, was nervous as she approached her annual meeting with her soccer coach, Anson Dorrance, before her sophomore season at the University of North Carolina[12]. He surprised her with a question. "What do you want this season?"

Mia was taken aback, but she quickly blurted out, "I want to be the best!"

Dorrance asked her what that meant, and Mia struggled to find an answer. He walked over to the light switch, turned it off and then back on, and said to her, "It's just a decision, but you have to make it every day." And he wisely left her to grapple with her truth.

Like most young adults, Mia had never really taken the time to go inward and figure out what *she* wanted, including why she wanted to play soccer. So much of many kids' motivation becomes not wanting to disappoint parents, teachers, coaches or teammates. Mia did some soul searching and decided she did want to be the best at her sport. She realized she had to choose between mediocrity and excellence, and that it was a decision she would have to make each and every day. Mia rededicated herself to put in the work to attain her goal with amazing results. She won four NCAA women's soccer championships, two World Cups and two Olympic gold medals in an illustrious career. Most importantly, she did it for her reasons.

When 13-year-old Taylor Swift took her songs to Nashville looking for a record deal, she was offered a development deal with RCA records, but they wanted her to record covers[13]. Taylor adamantly opted out because she was determined to only record her music. She instead signed with SONY/ATV as the youngest songwriter in the company's history. She resolutely declined help from adults who were more experienced because she wanted to do it her way. One of her handlers, Mark Tedder, remarked, "Artists who are the most successful are the ones who tell me to my face that I'm wrong about a song." Taylor did it her way to great success.

Brooke Lowrey, creator of an online clothing store called Brooklynn Street, told me she grew up wanting to be in control over what she was doing and that being unique was always important to her. School was too restricting for Brooke, and she never received affirmation for original thoughts. It was Brooke's rebellious spirit that got her in trouble for pushing the envelope, but it also taught her how to handle mistakes. "I was too stubborn to listen to other people, so I kind of always just did what I wanted," she said. "All of that trial and error taught me a lot about myself and what works for me. I trust myself and my decisions a lot more now because I know myself better." Brooke is a great example of someone who sets her own bar.

Emma, you may be receiving a lot of pressure to follow a safe path, and I know you care deeply about not wanting to disappoint people. It is so important at this juncture in your life to take some quiet, reflective time to make sure you are doing things for your reasons. Get clear about what success means for you, even if it goes against the grain. Everyone can 'have it all' as long as we are the ones who define what that means. Autonomy in choosing your path will lead to greater engagement, fulfillment and contentment. Set your own bar!

Much love and best birthday wishes,
Grandpa

Start of Senior Year:

⟶

What Motivates You?

Life was pretty good for Emma. She was living in an apartment with her three best friends, enjoying her psychology classes, and looking forward to a fun senior year of college. Driving back to college, she got the urge to read her grandfather's next letter, so she pulled over at the first truck stop and read his words.

Dearest Granddaughter,

So, you are starting the last leg of this part of your journey, college. Are you excited? Happy? Content? I hope so. I shared some thoughts in the last letter about setting your own bar, and as I was thinking about what you might need at this point in your life, I thought maybe a few ideas on motivation would be helpful. Let me first share a story about contentment and fulfillment.

People in a small town gathered every evening to make music together. There was a saxophonist, a violinist and a drummer, mostly elderly people. They got together for the company and for the sheer joy of making music, even if they didn't do it very well. They became best friends and greatly enjoyed their evenings together. That is, until the day they decided to get a conductor. This man had a lot of ambition and he told the group, "We have to have a concert, and we have to prepare a performance for the town." Gradually he got rid of some of the musicians who didn't play well, hired professional musicians, got the orchestra in shape, and they all got their names published in the local newspaper. At first it felt wonderful, so they decided to move to the big city and play there. But some of the old people had tears in their eyes, and they said, "It was so wonderful in the old days when we did things badly but enjoyed them immensely."[14]

When it comes to happiness and fulfillment, *why* you are doing something is more important than *what* you are doing. When the orchestra members' intention was to make music for the sake of the music and to have fun together with their friends, they derived a lot of joy and satisfaction from it. When their intention shifted to being the best, becoming famous and making money, the endeavor lost its fun and fulfillment.

In the last years of my life, I noticed families losing sight of what was really important, things like spending time together and relaxing. Everything became so competitive and intense. Parents were hyper-focused on their kids achieving top grades and being accepted into top-tier universities in order to get a lucrative job and make a lot of money. I used to dub this the 'money mantra.' Research has shown that people who are driven by externals like getting rich or becoming famous end up less happy and fulfilled, more depressed and stressed, and with poorer relationships in their lives compared to those focused on internal values such as societal contribution, personal growth and awareness, and healthy relationships. Having a lot of money or fame was not the problem; striving for materialistic things caused the damage.

I remember a point in my life where I felt empty and unhappy despite being successful. After giving a great talk in front of hundreds of people or running a life-changing retreat for adults, the applause and acknowledgments filled me up for a little while. But the empty feeling came back increasingly quicker. A mentor at the time, Bill Riedler, wisely told me that I didn't need to change what I was doing to become more happy and fulfilled, I just needed to switch *why* I was doing it. I was doing too many things for approval, to be applauded and to be better than others as a way to compensate for a childhood belief that I wasn't good enough. So I changed my intention from gaining applause and approval to being of service, and it made all the difference in the world. Focusing on making a difference redirected my motivation to more fulfilling values.

As you enter your final year of college, it is critical that you find your own motivation for doing everything in your life, as the well-known author Paulo Coelho did as a young man. Paulo was a boy who dreamed of becoming a writer. He grew up in Brazil under a repressive dictatorship that caused his parents to harbor many fears, and they lectured him that artists starve, drink and become homosexuals that are imprisoned. They were so upset by his thoughts of becoming a writer that they admitted him into a mental institution, and when he escaped and came home more determined than ever to write, they readmitted him twice more. It required a superhuman effort for Paulo to overcome all of this discouragement. It was his fierce love of the written word that motivated him to surpass incredible odds to become a best-selling author of books, including *The Alchemist.*

The amount of satisfaction you derive out of whatever you do is directly proportional to why you are doing it. If you have become motivated by not wanting to disappoint people, fame, becoming wealthy, or bolstering your image, it's time to switch your intentions to healthier reasons. Do not allow yourself to be driven by the narrow, prescribed path laid out by the money mantra. Higher-level intentions like being of service and making an impact on your community or the world will bring you the sense of freedom, happiness, and fulfillment you seek and deserve.

Those intentions fit perfectly with what I know about you as a person. You have always been the kind of person who was kind, caring and inclusive. You stood up for the underdog even when you were in kindergarten. My guess is that you will end up in some kind of helping profession, such as a doctor, nurse, therapist or teacher. Whatever career you choose, be conscious of your intentions for doing it. That's how you will end up happy and content.

Love and best wishes for a great year,
Grandpa

22ⁿᵈ Birthday:

Mistakes Won't Mess Up Your Life

Mistakes Won't Mess Up Your Life

Emma's senior year was flying by, and she was beginning to feel some angst about her plans after graduation. Like many of her peers, she had a belief that making a mistake in your 20s could mess up the rest of your life; missteps like: initially picking the wrong major in college; switching majors after a few years of study; moving to a big city for your first job and not making it; picking the wrong job out of college that you end up hating; missing out on job opportunities because you chose to travel abroad for a year; making a career change to follow a passion. Emma's fear that a decision that ends up not working out would derail her from a good life was causing her to hesitate sending out her resume to companies and grad schools, similar to her avoidant behaviors her senior year in high school. After her last class of the day, she curled up on the couch to read her grandfather's letter.

Happy birthday, Granddaughter!

Wow, 22 sounds a lot older than 21, doesn't it? I hope you are staying present and enjoying every moment of your final year in college. I know that big decisions are fast approaching, but I hope you don't let yourself get too stressed out. Too many young adults are hesitant to make life decisions because of their fear of making mistakes. The truth is that choices that don't work out at your age do not cripple you for the rest of your life. Every entrepreneur I know has experienced failures during their career, but they didn't let it limit their future. One of my best friends in college, Will, had a rough start in college, but he didn't allow it to ruin what came next.

Will wanted desperately to get a business degree, but he failed his calculus course three times, resulting in the dean of the business school suspending him from the university for a year. When he told his mom, her wise reply was, "Fix it." Will met with the dean and implored him to not put his education on hold for a year. The dean acquiesced by telling him he would only lift the suspension if Will could find another department to accept him. The only school to do so was speech and communications, where he subsequently majored in speech. Will says in retrospect, it was a great move because he learned vital skills like interviewing, interpersonal communication, debate, and how to best articulate ideas so others could understand. As the owner of seven businesses now, these skills have been invaluable in dealing with his employees and customers.

I have some homework for you, Emma. Interview adults and ask them about when they experienced mistakes, self-doubt and indecision. I promise you they will all have plenty of stories. Here is one about a man who went through a period of failure before he found his way.

Eminent journalist Tom Brokaw went through a tough time in his early 20s[15]. Things had always come easy to him as a star high school athlete, class president and student. After doing poorly his first year of college, he transferred to the University of South Dakota, where he proceeded to ignore his studies, chase girls and barely gain passing grades. The chair of the political science department invited him to dinner one evening and told him, "I've been thinking about you and what you're going to do with your life, and I think you should drop out. Get wine, women and song out of your system, and then come back when you're ready to do some good. Until then, I don't want to see you."

Tom's girlfriend dumped him, and he spent the next six months doing menial jobs in radio and TV. He remembers thinking, "I thought I could do anything I wanted on my own terms; I learned how wrong I had been." He begged his professor to take him back, which he did, but with some stipulations. "This time, it's on my terms. Here's your schedule, and here are the grades I expect you to get. You'll keep working full time at the jobs you have." Tom worked hard, earned his degree, married his old girlfriend, and went on to become a distinguished journalist and TV news anchor. "It was that painful time in my life, in which I was always adrift, that motivated me for years to come. It taught me how instructive a little failure at an early age can be."

I described the concept of 'going for the roar' in the letter for your first day of college, and it certainly applies here. Don't be afraid to take risks, challenge yourself, go against the grain, or change course midstream if your heart tells you to do so. Teach yourself to learn from mistakes and move on. This quote from Haruki Murakami comes to mind: "When you come out of the storm, you won't be the same person who walked in. That's what this storm's all about."

My dearest granddaughter, perhaps the best advice I can give you at this stage is to trust your gut about job decisions. Whatever choice you make, invest yourself fully in that endeavor, learn whatever new skills you can, and if you feel that it's time to move on, trust yourself. Have faith that you have the ability to overcome mistakes and failures and to create what you want. I've always believed in you, and I still do. I'll leave you with this quote that illustrates this point well.

"I know who I am today, yesterday, tomorrow. The world may be hard, it may be full of loss, but I believe in myself and what I'm doing. And that belief can carry me through the hard times; can allow me both a sense of purpose and a sense of joy." Victor Frankl

Much love and best birthday wishes, Grandpa

College Graduation:

Don't settle

Before you knew it, Emma was putting on her cap and gown and preparing to walk across the stage at her college graduation. The next leg of her journey included six months of traveling in Europe. People had been telling her all year that she would need a masters in her field of child psychology, but since she hadn't figured out yet what kind of work she wanted to do, grad school felt like it would be a waste of time and money. She had been working two jobs to save enough to travel, and her gut said that this time away would help her figure things out. Her grandfather's advice about being open to dots and following your heart had won out. Emma didn't want to rush into just anything and feel like she had settled. She wanted to be patient and trust in the process of life. She sat on the stoop of her apartment to read her grandfather's letter right before she left for the ceremony.

Dear College Graduate,

Congratulations on this big day. I so wish I could be there to see you cross that stage. I guess I'll have to cheer you on from this seat high above you. I wonder if you will be going directly out into the workforce or choosing to study more in grad school, or perhaps taking some time off to gather yourself. It seems to me that too many young people rush into jobs because of pressure from well-meaning people, and don't take time to reflect and relax. I've always been a big supporter of traveling to new places, especially if you can go without an agenda. You can learn a lot about yourself when you are truly flying by the seat of your pants.

Here are some questions I might have asked you if I was taking you out to dinner today. What do you want in life? What is your dream? Have you taken the time to filter out what everyone else thinks is right for you to figure out your truth? Have you decided yet that it's you, not your parents, professors or employers who must know what is in your best interests? Are you ready to commit to you?

Here is a great quote for you from Nelson Mandela: "There is no passion to be found playing small, in settling for a life that is less than the one you are capable of living."

If I was there today, I'd encourage you to forge your own path and to not settle. I remember watching a friend of mine's daughter, Amy, get locked into a full-time teaching job at a major university, but she still felt discontented. She shared with me that she had volunteered for several summers at a culinary camp for kids, and it was the only setting where she experienced total bliss. Amy felt so happy when she was connecting with the kids, and she felt her dream job would be to work in an elementary school teaching cooking and nutrition. She actually was offered such a job right after finishing her masters but decided not to take it because it only paid half the salary of a master's level registered dietitian. Amy gave up on her dream of working with kids because she had this sense that she was supposed to grow up and get a real job with a good income. I hope you don't settle in this way, and that you are supported to follow your passions.

Jane Goodall, the eminent primatologist, had a mother who supported her crazy love of animals. When she expressed her dream of going to Africa as a 10-year-old, everyone laughed at her except her mom, who encouraged her with these words, "If you really want something, you must be prepared to work very hard, take advantage of all opportunities, and above all else, never give up." I echo these words to you.

I can remember young adults I counseled telling me that their parents wouldn't pay for their college if they went into elementary education because teaching jobs wouldn't pay enough to support them. One parent even refused to pay for her daughter's education degree because, in her parent's words, "You have more potential than that." I hated hearing that kind of discouragement. Too many young people give up on their dreams of becoming artists, teachers, dancers, beauticians, poets and songwriters because well-meaning adults have dissuaded them; don't let that be you. The duckling in the following story stayed true to her calling.

A duck's egg somehow found its way under a hen. When it hatched, the duckling followed the mother hen around the barnyard just like the baby chicks. One day they walked by a lake, whereupon the duckling went straight into the water and swam about. The mother hen remained clucking anxiously on the shore, pleading to the duckling to come back ashore.

Like the duckling, you may choose a path that frightens others because it is out of their comfort zone. They may not be able to support you because they come from a different place. Remaining on the shore to appease other people is a surefire way to keep the status quo, but the cost is that you will settle into someone else's version of your destiny, and misery will follow. Remember Bobbi Brown's powerful quote from your junior year letter: "There are so many options for how you live your life and make a career for yourself. If you can identify and stick with something you're genuinely passionate about, you're ahead of the game. You'll figure out how to make money once you figure out what you love to do."

In a previous letter, I wrote about Paul Coelho, the author of the book *The Alchemist*. He had to overcome being admitted into an insane asylum three times by his parents in order to pursue his dream of being a writer. I know that you, too, have that kind of determination. Be conscious of why you are making decisions along your career path, as many people get derailed from pursuing jobs and experiences that bring them joy and fulfillment, and end up gaining the world and losing their souls.

If your heart is guiding you to becoming something that is unpopular, nontraditional, doesn't pay as well or isn't valued by other people, stay strong and follow your bliss. Don't settle into someone else's idea of what is right for you. You are the captain of your ship.

I'll leave you with this beautiful poem, *Invictus*, from William Ernest Henley:

> *Out of the night that covers me, black as the pit from pole to pole*
> *I thank whatever gods may be, for my unconquerable soul.*
> *In the fell clutch of circumstance, I have not winced nor cried aloud*
> *Under the bludgeoning of fate, my head is bloody, but unbowed.*
> *Beyond this place of wrath and tears,*
> *looms but the horror of the shade.*
> *And yet, the menace of the years finds, and shall find me, unafraid.*
> *It matters not how strait the gate,*
> *how charged with punishment the scroll*
> *I am the master of my fate – I am the captain of my soul.*

Congratulations on a job well done!
Love, Grandpa

23rd Birthday:

ح

Unrevealed Commitments

What a whirlwind year it had been for Emma. She spent a week at home relaxing after graduation, bought a backpack and supplies, and then took off for Europe. She had decided to go solo because she wanted some quiet, alone time to really be with herself. Being alone was unsettling at first, and she became homesick by week two. The hard-charging Emma also began to doubt the whole idea of the trip, feeling like a slacker. But she stuck it out, and by the end of the first month, she had found her rhythm. Her confidence grew as she handled every challenge that crossed her path. By trip's end, Emma had developed the firm belief that no matter what, she had the ability to make anything happen. She was more committed than ever that she wanted to make a difference in the lives of children.

Upon arrival home, she found a job working as a mentor for girls in an inner city high school. She loved the girls she worked with and became aware that she had some holes in her training that could be filled by a local university master's program. By the time her 23rd birthday rolled around, Emma felt like she had grown a ton since her grandfather's last letter.

Dear Emma,

I hope this letter finds you happy and content on this, your 23rd birthday. I also hope you have found some direction as far as your calling. This is an important time in your life to keep acquiring dots, even if the final picture of your life's work hasn't emerged yet. As young adults approach their mid-to-late 20s, they sometimes start to feel like things aren't working out for them or they keep falling short in achieving important goals. I've heard people complain that they aren't getting a committed romantic partner, the closeness they desire in a relationship, a job or promotion they think they deserve, or the respect they want from friends or co-workers. A common reaction to this frustration is to blame everybody and everything around you, which leaves you angry, resentful and harboring a victim mentality. People can remain stuck with this mindset for a lifetime if they don't wake up to reality.

I learned an invaluable metaphor years ago from a mentor, Bill Reidler. Imagine that you are shooting arrows at a target, but they keep falling short of the mark. The target represents the goal you are striving for, but since you continue to miss the mark, it indicates that there must be something more important than the perceived goal. There is something below your level of awareness causing the misfire, a subconscious motive you are more committed to than achieving the goal. I like to call these unrevealed commitments, and they can take on all kinds of forms. What can become more important than getting what you want is playing it safe because of a fear of making mistakes or failing; being in control; being more committed to being right than being close; pleasing others or not disappointing others; staying in your comfort zone to avoid discomfort; or not wanting to grow up and take responsibility for your life.

Remember the story about me I shared in the senior year letter? I thought I was focused on helping people in my talks and retreats, but the result was a sense of emptiness. I became aware that what I was more committed to was getting applause and other people's approval. I switched my intention to being that of service, and the result was more joy and gratification.

People can remain stuck in unfulfilling patterns because they lack awareness of what is subconsciously driving them, their unrevealed commitments. You may not have gotten to this frustrating point, and I hope you never do. Staying on target to achieve your true goals requires being aware of your motivations and intentions in every moment.

My dear Emma, if you ever feel that you are missing the mark, step back from your life and figure out your actual commitment. Unrevealed commitments only hold power over your results if they remain unconscious. Shine the light of awareness on them and soar.

This is such an exciting time in your life, hopefully full of new friends, new challenges, new dots and perhaps new places to live. I'll visit you with one more letter on your 25th birthday to help you celebrate the quarter mark of your life. Until then, try to be in the moment, be open to dots, savor each moment, go for the roar, focus on your positive wolf, be compassionate with yourself, and keep trusting your gut and heart when it comes to life decisions. I have full faith that you are unfolding amazingly just like the beautiful roses I used to grow. Oh, and stop and smell the roses, too.

Love, Grandpa

Final Letter:

⸻

Open When Needed

The final letter on the bottom of the box had just two words written on the envelope: 'When needed.' Emma kept the box in her desk drawer, figuring she'd pull it out when she was having a bad day. But as the months went by, she forgot about it. She was still working full-time as a mentor for disadvantaged girls in an inner city high school, and she was taking three classes each semester in grad school.

Despite her hectic schedule, Emma had still managed to have a boyfriend, Ted, for 10 months. The relationship was not going well, and it seemed they were arguing over everything. He complained a lot about her not having enough time for him, and so he was going out to the bars with his friends more. Seeing him on social media with girls hanging on him at parties drove her crazy. The kids at school were incredibly challenging, and the administration didn't offer her any support. The morale of the staff was low, making it a pretty toxic environment. It also was becoming a chore to go to classes three evenings a week, and she wasn't enjoying it as much as she had anticipated. All of this had Emma doubting her job, decisions and most importantly, doubting herself.

Feeling stressed out and overwhelmed, she thought of her grandfather and missed his reassurance more than ever. That's when she remembered the last letter. She took it to bed that night, and even just seeing his scribbly handwriting made her smile. Emma was surprised to also find a CD in the envelope with her name written on it. Her curiosity was aroused.

Dear Granddaughter,

It saddens me to think that you need this letter, and that I can't physically be there when you are hurting. But I have one final gift for you that I hope will take care of that problem. You see, you really can visit with me, just in a different way than we'd both like. I guess you noticed the CD by now. Knowing that you'd hit a few bumps in the road, I recorded my voice doing a visualization as a way to have conversations together. Download it to your phone, relax, and follow along with my voice before you read any further.

Emma quickly downloaded the visualization, closed her eyes and pressed play. Her grandfather's soothing voice was just the tonic she needed.

Hey, Emma. I want you to close your eyes and follow along with my voice. Take a couple of slow, deep breaths like I taught you many years ago and relax. Imagine that you are walking on our favorite trail in the woods on a bright, sunny day. See yourself walk into that clearing that has the big, white, flat rock we used to sit on, and see yourself going there and sitting down. Then notice me walking out of the forest and sitting beside you. We greet each other with a big hug, and then it's time for one of our talks. You can ask me how I'm doing, update me on your life, ask me questions, ask for advice, whatever you want.

So Emma did just that. She told him through tears about her lack of support at school, how toxic the school staff had become, her lack of motivation for grad school and about the troubles in her relationship with Ted. Emma told him she wondered if she would ever have her life together. In her mind, she saw her grandfather listening intently as he always had, and it felt so good to be heard and understood. He reassured her that most people in their 20s have ups and downs and moments of indecision and self-doubt. He also reminded her that he hadn't really found himself and his calling until his early 30s.

He asked Emma if she wanted a suggestion about her relationship, and she said yes. Her grandpa told her that romantic relationships at her age should not be so hard. Of course there are disagreements that need to be worked through, and times when one person has more energy for the relationship. But if in the early going it feels hard and draining, his advice to her was to get out of the relationship and move on.

Emma next asked him what she should do about her job and grad school. In her visualization, grandpa asked her to get in touch with what brought her the most joy; who was there, where was she, what was she doing. She thought about it for a moment, and her mind went back to a week she had spent last summer as a camp counselor at Camp Weloki for Girls. She loved sitting in the group circles helping the teen girls process through challenges they were facing. She loved the way every member of the staff was seen as valuable, and how they worked in harmony. At the end of that week, she felt like she had finally found her 'tribe.' And that's when it hit Emma that what she really loved was working with groups of teens, not one-on-one. Her camp week had been an amazing 'dot' for her. With that piece in place, she told her grandfather she now knew what kind of training and education she would need for that kind of work.

In her visualization, it was time to say goodbye. Emma thanked her grandpa for being there for her, and he promised that she could always call him to mind for a talk. They gave each other a long, warm embrace, and then he got up and walked back into the forest. She sensed a peace that she hadn't felt in a long time. She slowly opened her eyes and came back to the present moment in her bedroom. Emma picked up the letter and resumed reading.

Well granddaughter, I hope that little visit together brought you some peace of mind with your struggles. I strongly encourage you to develop the ability to have quiet, alone time for reflection. That is the only way to discover what you want and need, and to uncover your deepest desires and passions. It's hard to set your own bar and find your path if, like Mia Hamm, you haven't looked within for those answers.

I hope your life is full of adventures, and that you have the courage to forge your own path. I heard a story once about a group of tourists who were traveling on a bus through the beautiful Tuscany countryside. Surprisingly, all of the window shades were pulled down so that no one could see beyond the windows. The travelers spent the whole trip arguing over who got to sit in front, who deserved a window seat and who was in charge, and who was to be admired. And so they remained until journey's end. Those tourists were sleepwalking through life and had no awareness of it. It reminds me of the old saying, "Life is a banquet, and yet most people are starving." My wish for you is that you savor each moment and live your life consciously, wide awake and fully present.

I also hope you can let go of feeling so much stress and anxiety about having it all figured out. Remind yourself that you are right on track for your own timeline, and stop trying to force life. The following story by Dorothy Mince might help you relax about not being behind others: *A young girl grew impatient waiting for a rosebud to unfold in her grandfather's garden. Her grandpa told her that if she couldn't hold off, to go ahead and unfold the petals. When the girl had done so, she was disappointed to see that there was no beautiful rose as she had imagined. She had actually destroyed its beauty, and the flower quickly withered and died. Her wise grandfather then explained that it was thus with all things; we must let them unfold in their own way and in their own time.*

I will continue watching as you grow into the beautiful, strong, courageous, compassionate woman I know you are. But don't forget to let your mischievous, silly little girl come out to play sometimes, too. Trust your gut and go after experiences you are drawn to that seem fun, even if it is unconventional. Use the stories from my letters, biographies you read, or stories from adults you know to build confidence that dots will connect, and that life will unfold for you. Perhaps instead of anxiously trying to find your calling, you patiently allow your calling to find you. I'll leave you with one of my favorite quotes from one of my favorite authors, Anthony De Mello, that describes well this process of trusting in life.

"The desire to change is the enemy of love. Don't change yourself, love yourself as you are. Don't try to change others, love them as they are. Don't try to change the world, it's in God's hands and he knows. And if you do this, change will occur, marvelously, in its own way and in its own time. Yield to the current of life, unencumbered by baggage."

I love you and am always here for you in memories, spirit and in your heart. Stay in touch.

Love, Grandpa

Notes For Chapters

1. Information, please: Paul Villard: Originally published June, 1966 Readers Digest; reprinted with permission in the December 1999 issue of the *Singing Wires* newsletter, TCI club.

2. Nathan Sawaya story: https://www.npr.org/2014/03/20/291482148/nathan-sawaya-lego-my-van-gogh

3. Artist's iconic sculptures are made with Legos: Diane Toroian Keaggy; *St. Louis Post Dispatch* Sept. 23, 2012

4. Jennifer Lawrence story adapted from piece on 60 Minutes Show aired February 25, 2018

5. *Jim Henson, The Biography*; Brian Jay Jones, Ballantine Books, 2013

6. *Sports Illustrated* December 14, 2015; Alexander Wolff article on Becky Hammon

7. Adapted from story in the book, *The Element*, Ken Robinson, Viking Penguin, 2009

8. Bobbi Brown story adapted from *Where You Go Is Not Who You'll Be*, Frank Bruni, Grand Central Publishing 2015

9. Sharon Long story adapted from *Callings; The Purpose and Passion of Work*, Dave Isay, Penguin Press, 2016

10. Dorothy Wharburton story adapted from *Callings; The Purpose and Passion of Work*, Dave Isay, Penguin Press, 2016

11. Nicole Hanton story adapted from *The Right Words at the Right Time Volume 2*, Marlo Thomas; Atria Books 2006

12. Mia Hamm story adapted from *The Right Words at the Right Time*. Marlo Thomas, Atria Books, 2002

13. Taylor Swift story adapted from article: "The Power of Taylor Swift", Jack Dickey, Time Magazine November 24, 2014

14. Orchestra story adapted from *Awareness*, Anthony De Mello, Doubleday 1990

15. Tom Brokaw story adapted from *The Right Words at the Right Time*, Marlo Thomas, Atria Books, 2002

Acknowledgments

I have several people I wish to acknowledge for their help in getting this book written. First and foremost, my wife Anne. She tends to cringe when I tell her I'm starting a new venture, but as the President of our company she handles all of the day-to-day details that allow me to focus on creating new things, like this book. My three children, Kelly, TJ, and John and my son-in-law Steve have also always been supportive of my new undertakings, and especially now as young adults.

I'm also grateful for all of my 'editors', people who gave me feedback along the way. My son John and his fiancée Isa were brutally honest all along the way, and they helped me focus and hone in on what I really wanted to say. I could not have done this without their constant advice. I also want to thank several other young adults who let me bounce ideas off of them: Brooke Lowrey, Christina Mason, Emma Bliss, Emma Campbell, Chris Fuchs, Kavita Krell, and Maddie Cofer. And of course, a big thanks to my real editor Karyn Williams from Town and Style magazine who made the book much easier to read.

Cathy Davis and her team at Davis Creative did a great job of getting the book ready for publishing and publishing it as well. Thanks so much for taking on my project.

I have had so many incredible mentors along the way: pre-med advisor Brother John Donahoo, residency director Reed Bell M.D., fellowship directors Chris Williams M.D. and T. Berry Brazelton M.D., authors Anthony De Mello and Eknath Easwaran, Bill Reidler and Kath Kvols. I'm eternally grateful to some of my dear friends with whom I've had so many deep conversations about life and whom I've bounced ideas off of for years: Dave and Liz Fuchs, John and Gail Strubberg, and Russ and Jan Loida. I hope that everyone reading this book experiences support like I did.

Lastly, I want to give a huge shout-out to all of the kids, teenagers, and millennials who have opened up and shared their stories to me in my counseling practice, weekend retreats, summer camps, and workshops around the world over the past 28 years. Much of what I know about young adults comes from listening to you in our sharing circles. I heard your needs, and hope I have met some of them with the wisdom in these pages. You continue to inspire me.

About the Author

Tim Jordan M.D is a developmental and behavioral pediatrician who studied with Dr. T. Berry Brazelton at Harvard Medical School. He has worked with teenagers and 20-somethings for over 30 years in his counseling practice and in his personal growth/leadership development weekend retreats and summer camps. Dr. Jordan was inspired to write this book after sitting in circles with hundreds of young adults listening to their experiences and supporting them through the challenges of becoming successful adults. He is also a popular blogger, podcaster, and media consultant.

He and his wife Anne have been married for 37 years and have 3 adult children and one grandson. Dr. Jordan is an avid reader, loves the outdoors and traveling, and is a master storyteller.

Visit his website at www.drtimjordan.com for details about his books, blogs, podcasts, retreats and camps.

You can contact Dr. Jordan at drtimjordanmedia@gmail.com